ON DOUBT

Leigh Sales

MELBOURNE
UNIVERSITY
PRESS

MELBOURNE UNIVERSITY PRESS
An imprint of Melbourne University Publishing Limited
187 Grattan Street, Carlton, Victoria 3053, Australia
mup-info@unimelb.edu.au
www.mup.com.au

First published 2009
Text © Leigh Sales, 2009
Design and typography © Melbourne University Publishing Limited,
2009

Text design by Alice Graphics
Cover design by Nada Backovic Design
Typeset by TypeSkill
Printed in Australia by Griffin Press, SA

National Library of Australia Cataloguing-in-Publication entry

Sales, Leigh.
On doubt / Leigh Sales.

9780522856040 (hbk.)

Belief and doubt.
Self-doubt.
Skepticism.

121.5

The beginning of wisdom is found in doubting; by doubting we come to the question, and by seeking we may come upon the truth.

Pierre Abelard, French philosopher, teacher and theologian, 1079–1142

I

On the first day of primary school each year, my mother would deliver me to my new teacher with the same introduction. 'If she's any trouble,' Mum would say with a pointed stare in my direction, 'please give her a thrashing and then send her home with a note so that I know to give her another one'.

Authority was to be respected. It would have been unthinkable to call my school friends' parents by their first names as children do today. And if we visited somebody's home with Mum and Dad, we were to sit quietly until invited to do otherwise. No matter how much my fingers itched to touch their piano, no matter that I was dying to make their cockatoo talk, no matter that I remembered from the previous visit that there was a calendar in the toilet showing cartoons of famous people with enormous private parts: I would not dare move until given permission.

I remember a child once came to our place and demanded some cordial by simply barking, 'Cordy!' My brother and I couldn't have been more than four and five, but I still recall the way our heads snapped up and the look of horror we gave each other. Imagine! Going to a stranger's house and asking for a drink before one was offered—and not even saying *please*!

Discipline was strict in our house and there was no more powerful tool than Mum's threat, 'I'll tell your father when he gets home'. Dad was an infantryman, a regimental sergeant major by the time I was a teenager. You could see your face in his boots, and your life flashing before you in his eyes. Like most people in his line of work, the sound of his raised voice crossed a chainsaw with a starving grizzly bear.

Dad and I had a volatile relationship. Although I was generally well behaved in public, I was a bit of a handful at home, mostly because I insisted on questioning everything. Dad was accustomed to giving orders to soldiers all day and being silently obeyed. Seemingly from the cradle, I had an uncontrollable urge to respond to all his directives with 'But why?' At the end of a dressing-down, he would roar, 'Do you understand?' I would, somewhat unwisely, often pick him up on a point or two, seeking clarification.

Surprisingly, my parents did not find this at all endearing. I recall one tea time when Dad, boiling with rage, slammed his hands down on the table, gripped its edges, looked skyward as if to God and with a shaking voice spluttered, 'Give me strength!' On another occasion, I drove Mum to such fury that she tipped a drink over my head. If I were sent to my room—

a common outcome—I would wail and weep as if the world were ending.

I found it hardest to hold my tongue when, in my immense eleven-year-old wisdom, I considered my parents' logic to be flawed. My brother and I fought constantly, and I particularly chafed at Mum's decree that we deserved equal punishment because 'it takes two to fight'.

'It doesn't take two!' I would cry indignantly, when hauled to my bedroom. 'It takes one! It takes him, coming in here and slapping me when all I was doing was reading my book!' I was a long, skinny kid with limbs like tentacles, and I'd resist all the way, wrapping a foot around a table leg or winding an arm through a chair. As Mum tried to stuff me into my room like a pair of shoes into an over-packed suitcase, I'd rant, 'Why are you saying that it takes two? You can't explain it because you know it doesn't make sense!'

My backchat and constant questions didn't stem from rebellion alone. I was curious about everything. Until I was about thirteen, I shared a room with my Nana, my mother's mother, who lived with us. There were few worse sins in her book than being 'a stickybeak'. She had a visceral loathing of one of our neighbours, and as best I could tell, the woman's only crime was that she was apparently a stickybeak who wore too much jewellery. My father was also frequently accused of stickybeaking. 'He has eyes like a hawk',

Nana would rail, by no means intending it as a compliment.

Nana perhaps didn't realise that she was sleeping next to the biggest stickybeak in the house. I was a chronic eavesdropper. I loved to listen to my mother on the phone with her friends, and would find any excuse to skulk around the conversation. At night, after I'd been ordered to bed, I would press my ear to the bedroom wall, straining to hear *Prisoner* on the television set in the lounge room. Even though the program scared me witless, I couldn't bear not knowing what was happening. At school, I'd just about burst with satisfaction at discovering a teacher's first name. 'It's not Mrs Canterutti', I'd run and tell my best friend breathlessly. 'It's *Vicki*!'

Nana was a great reader of women's magazines, and I swiped them obsessively to read the advice columns. I loved them all, indiscriminately consuming advice on medical issues, parenting, sex and relationships. I was oddly ashamed of this habit and would hide in the toilet with Nana's treasure-trove, sneakily devouring people's stories and lapping up the columnists' suggestions. To this day, the addiction persists. Every day, I go to salon. com and read 'Since you asked'. I'm also enamoured of 'Dear Prudence: advice on morals and manners' on slate.com. When I lived in the USA, I used to pick up a weekly local newspaper solely to read

'Savage Love', a hysterically funny column on kinky sexual problems.

The pleasures of Dan Savage's biting wit, though, were a long way from my childhood home in the Pine Rivers shire on the outskirts of Brisbane. A fellow politician once accused the Prime Minister, Queenslander Kevin Rudd, of joking that after you cross the Pine Rivers, 'you can hear the sound of banjo music', a reference to the creepy rednecks in the 1972 film *Deliverance*. (Mr Rudd denies it.)

There were no banjos in my parents' modest house, and none of us had six fingers, but the moral code was built on traditional foundations of hard work and good manners, and was strictly enforced. My parents instilled in me the classic

Protestant work ethic, although they were entirely uninterested in religion, if not overtly hostile. Mum had attended Catholic schools and decided that she didn't want her children 'brainwashed'. Accordingly, she instructed our state school principal that my brother and I were to be sent to the library during the weekly religious education class.

Mum's anti-church streak bred in me an intense curiosity about religion. A few weeks after I finished grade 12, a good friend invited me to his church youth group. It started an association with Christianity that lasted several years. I attended a Pentecostal church affiliated with Hillsong, offering slick music and lots of young devotees. The church's social scene was engaging, and the Bible was interesting reading. But by my early twenties, I had serious doubts about religion, and soon after, I abandoned it altogether. My problem was not a lack of effort or a lack of desire to believe. The problem for me was a lack of faith: how do I *know* this is true?

From almost the first day I attended church, my questions started. They were the same ones that drum away at all atheists and agnostics: How do I know God exists? How do I know the Bible is true? What is the hard evidence for this? Many of my questions concerned fairness: Is it really the case that people who don't believe all this are going to hell? Doesn't that seem a bit harsh?

I sincerely wanted to be free of my inconvenient questions, but I needed answers based in reason, evidence and logic. I pored over the Bible, and I asked church leaders and friends. Their answers were always along the lines of 'You just need to let it go and have faith' or 'Because it's in the Bible'. That was profoundly unsatisfactory—the equivalent of my parents' mantra 'Because I say so'.

Ultimately, religious faith eluded me. Perhaps a fundamentalist church was not for somebody with my quirks. It was uncompromising: you either believed the dogma and had admission to heaven or indulged doubt and 'chipped away at your own salvation', as one pastor memorably put it to me. Whatever the reason,

I could not bring myself to say, 'I believe in something for which there is no irrefutable proof, yet in spite of that, I am so certain of my own opinion that I can declare that you are going to hell for not sharing it'. Atheism struck me as being just as unattractive as Christianity. It too required a leap of faith to a position of certainty, albeit in the opposite direction.

The only thing in which I found faith was doubt. It struck me as a far more natural state of being. Faith required effort that was beyond me. Doubt was instinctive. This mentality spread well beyond my attitude to religion and into politics. If somebody subscribed doggedly to a particular political ideology, it struck me that they were constrained by it.

My doubts were also personal and directed inwards: *Am I good enough? Am I smart enough? Am I pretty enough? Am I doing the right thing?* If I were offered an opportunity, it was normal to wonder, *Am I up to this?* I admired well-grounded confidence in others, but I felt that people with unwavering certainty in themselves, and in their beliefs and opinions, suffered from a form of moral vanity. I found it an unattractive trait, and I didn't want to be like that. I also feared that I would never genuinely learn anything if I started from a mind-set of certainty. And I liked learning more than almost anything else. Journalism seemed an obvious career choice. I assumed it was a job in which a doubtful mind would be a professional asset.

II

Most of us tend to consider ourselves 'normal', whether we are or not. We judge the behaviour of other people in comparison with ourselves. This means I've always regarded self-doubt in others as entirely understandable, and extreme confidence as a mystery. In 2008, I was fascinated by the self-assurance of Sarah Palin, the Republican Party's vice presidential candidate in the US election. When the

Republican nominee, John McCain, asked Palin to be his running mate, she leapt right in:

> I didn't hesitate. I answered him yes because I have the confidence in that readiness and knowing that you can't blink, that you have to be wired in a way of being so committed to the mission, the mission that we're on, reform of this country and victory in this war, you can't blink, so I didn't blink then, even when he asked me to run as his running mate.

I envied Palin's chutzpah. Where did it come from? It certainly wasn't based on relevant experience. The feisty mother of five had been the mayor of the tiny Alaskan town of Wasilla for six years, and then the state's governor for twenty-one months. She had no foreign-policy credentials and no federal political experience. Yet with her nation ensnared in two complicated wars abroad and on the brink of economic disaster, Palin didn't 'blink' about becoming Vice President to a 72-year-old whose past health problems included cancer. The idea that she had not entertained even a moment of self-doubt astonished me. Was it because she genuinely possessed such confidence? Or was it because, in our society, to publicly admit doubt is becoming impossible?

By the time Sarah Palin appeared on the world political stage, I had been a journalist for sixteen years. I only knew how to do the job one way, and that was to approach everything with respectful scepticism. My childhood tendency to backchat carried through into adulthood. The more passionate or certain an interviewee was about an issue, the more it rankled me and the more I wanted to pick. I tried to temper my ingrained contrariness with good manners, as Mum and Dad had drilled into me. My reporting wasn't perfect, and I learnt on the job, but I considered my doubtful mind useful because it enabled me to skip easily from one side of an argument to another.

In recent times, my doubts have come to focus on my own approach to journalism. At some time in the future, will my mind-set make me a dinosaur? In the media and politics today, certainty has more cachet than doubt. This age of cable television and internet blogs seems to have spawned a growing number of people who think that their own opinions are always right and that those who disagree are not only wrong but worthy of contempt. Any admission of doubt or display of indecision is interpreted as weakness. I've always thought being a fence-sitter is a good thing for a journalist. But is it going out of vogue? The case of Sarah Palin is one of many recent episodes to give me pause.

Palin's appearance in the US election campaign was a gift for partisan commentators on both sides of the political divide. They could not have come up with better fodder for their 'culture wars' if they had invented her themselves. The moose-shooting, God-fearing, pro-life former beauty queen played beautifully into the simplified conflict cultivated by the partisan pundits who dominate talk radio, newspaper opinion pages, cable talk shows and blogs. Palin was underqualified for the role of Vice President. That was not to say she was stupid or incapable, but any examination of her work history and the duties of a Vice President showed that she sorely lacked relevant experience. Reaching this conclusion was not indicative of left-wing bias. It was an opinion held by many conservatives, including the former secretary of state Colin Powell, writers Kathleen Parker, David Brooks, Charles

Krauthammer and Andrew Sullivan, and former Bush speechwriter David Frum. 'I think she has pretty thoroughly—and probably irretrievably—proven that she is not up to the job of being President of the United States', Frum told the *New York Times* shortly after Palin gave a rambling, and at times incoherent, interview to American journalist Katie Couric.

Despite this, rational discussion about Palin's lack of qualifications was almost impossible from the start because her defenders tied criticism of her to ideology. They could not address the matter of her inexperience head-on, so they shifted the goalposts. She's inexperienced? So is Barack Obama! She lacks readiness? Stop being sexist! Her interviews show she is out of her depth? That's the bias of the East Coast liberal media elite and their 'gotcha journalism'.

Columnist Melanie Phillips, in the United Kingdom's *Daily Mail* news-paper, mounted a predictable right-wing defence:

> Not only is she young, attractive, clever, witty and feisty; her love for her Down's Syndrome baby embodies hope for the future. As for her pregnant 17-year-old daughter's proposed shotgun wedding, the priority there is the welfare of the unborn child. By contrast, the 'right to choose' feminist Left, which also thinks all women have a right to deprive a baby of its father, appears not just callous and selfish, but even downright murderous.

Which is why so called 'progressives' on both sides of the Atlantic have gone into paroxysms of rage and panic over Sarah Palin.

Palin's detractors on the Left weren't exactly subdued either. Here is the *New York Times*' Maureen Dowd:

Enthusiastic Republicans don't see the choice of Palin as affirmative action, despite her thin résumé and gaping absence of foreign policy knowledge, because they expect Republicans to put an underqualified 'babe', as Rush Limbaugh calls her, on the ticket. They have a tradition of nominating fun, bantamweight cheerleaders from the West, like the previous Miss

Congeniality types Dan Quayle and W, and then letting them learn on the job. So they crash into the globe a few times while they're learning to drive, what's the big deal?

Perhaps nobody turns to Melanie Phillips or Maureen Dowd looking for objective analysis. Readers know that these pundits hold strong political views and read them to feel either affirmed or outraged—or perhaps just entertained. We have similar writers and broadcasters in Australia: Andrew Bolt, Phillip Adams, Piers Akerman, Mike Carlton and Alan Jones, to name a few. Many of these commentators can be witty and engaging. Hidden within the unapologetically one-sided diatribes are often nuggets of insight.

There is certainly a place for these voices. But what worries me is that, increasingly, they set the tone for, and lead, the public discourse. In decades past, the heroes of journalism—even on opinion pages—were the voices of reason and cool authority, journalists such as Walter Cronkite, Edward R Murrow and Walter Lippman. Now, in the twenty-first century, one of the surest paths to media stardom is to shout more inflammatory invective louder than anybody else. The greater the reaction that commentators provoke, and the more traffic they attract to their publications or broadcasts, the higher their profiles and the fatter their pay cheques. There is obviously a skill to identifying hot-button issues and sparking debate. But when public debate is all sound and fury, where can we go for nuanced thinking and genuine illumination? Some of Australia's highest-profile commentators are people who act—in public at least—as if they have never experienced a second of self-doubt or entertained the thought that they might be wrong.

The worst commentary in Australia is more concerned with point-scoring than with educating audiences. Some commentators play to their own cliques, neglecting the wider public. They tend to exaggerate the facts or selectively highlight those that support their own positions, while conveniently ignoring those that do not. They do not realise—or perhaps care—that by overstating an argument, they undermine it. Opponents' views are taken out of context or subtly skewed to distort them, and any error, no matter how tiny, is magnified in an attempt to discredit the whole. Thoughtful opinion writers, both conservative and liberal, occasionally disagree with those of the same stripe. But the commentary that bothers me toes the ideological line unswervingly, regardless of the contortions of logic required. As the polemicist Hendrik Hertzberg observes, 'A political ideology is a very handy thing to have.

It's a real time-saver, because it tells you
what you think about things you know
nothing about'.

Modern commentary can also display
a striking lack of civility. It's not enough
to politely disagree; opponents must be
ridiculed, personally vilified and treated as
genuine enemies. The tone often reeks of
an unappealing moral certitude. Perhaps
this has always been the case and I've
not noticed it. I suspect, though, that the
internet and cable television have fuelled a
change of tone. During the 1960s, two of
the era's highest-profile ideological opponents were the radical left-wing writer
Normal Mailer and the famous conservative and founder of *National Review*,
William F Buckley. The *New Yorker*

recently published a letter from Mailer to Buckley, dating from January 1966:

Dear Bill,

I send you the enclosed not because I love *National Review* so much, for I don't—it's not so good as it ought to be, and often it's tiresome, especially when one knows in advance what your trusted old line contributors are going to say—but as a personal mark of respect to you. Your letter was the best letter I ever read by an editor asking for funds …

One request. Please keep my contribution in the secret crypts. It is not that I fear public opinion so much as ceaseless repetition. Repetition kills the soul and I would not wish to spend one hundred evenings in succession explaining to various outraged and somewhat stupid people in calm clear fashion my complex motives for giving a gift to a magazine for which I feel no affection and to an editor with whom on ninety of a hundred points I must rush to disagree. They would not understand that good writing is good writing and occasionally carries the day.

Yours,
Norman.

The recent experience of William F Buckley's son, the writer Christopher Buckley, illustrates how the nature of public debate has perhaps changed from the father's generation to the son's. The younger Buckley, who is also a conservative, wrote an article endorsing Democrat Barack Obama for the US presidency entitled 'Sorry, Dad, I'm Voting for Obama'. He argued that John McCain had lost his authenticity and political courage during the election campaign, abandoning principle for opportunism, particularly with the Sarah Palin choice. By contrast, Buckley believed that Obama had demonstrated a first-class temperament and intellect. Although Buckley was a permanent contributor to his father's magazine, he chose to publish the piece on a website, the *Daily Beast*, fearing a backlash against *National Review* if it ran his column. Despite Buckley's best efforts,

both *National Review* and he were deluged
with hate mail. Buckley decided he had no
option but to resign from the magazine to
'protect its future'. In a second post on the
Daily Beast, he expressed 'a certain sad-
ness that an act of publishing a reasoned
argument for the opposition should result
in acrimony and disavowal'.

This polarised and vitriolic intellectual
environment is not unique to the USA.
In Australia, it is similar, if not worse.
Australia is a far smaller nation than the
USA, so we have fewer voices to balance
the shouters. There can also be a nasty
personal element and a tendency towards
vendetta in some Australian commentary
that I rarely recall encountering in the

best American newspapers. Here, commentators attack each other by name for daring to hold contrary views.

In 2008, the conservative Australian commentator Gerard Henderson and the liberal academic Robert Manne engaged in a tit-for-tat exchange that perplexed me when the men made it public. Manne and Henderson became embroiled in a dispute about a piece Manne had written for the *Monthly* about radical journalist Wilfred Burchett. Henderson took issue with one paragraph in an essay of a dozen or so pages, believing it inaccurately alleged that Henderson (among others) had lent support to the massacre of thousands of communists in Indonesia in the 1960s. Manne disagreed, claiming that Henderson had taken the sentence referring to himself out of context. Thus began an exchange in which two of Australia's leading public intellectuals traded more than ten thousand words of insult and vitriol via email, which each then published in print or online. Yet, as the *Australian* newspaper pointed out, they actually agreed with each other on the salient point of the original piece: that Burchett was a communist, on the wrong side during the Cold War.

Henderson published most of the emails in the *Sydney Institute Quarterly*, and Manne then reproduced the whole lot on the *Monthly*'s website. Here is a taste of Manne's introduction:

It is published, not mainly as a comment on the ethical standards of the Director of the Sydney Institute [Henderson], nor even as evidence of his legalistic pedantry, evasiveness, disingenuousness and intellectual shallowness. All this is too well known to require demonstration. It is published, rather, because, strangely enough, so far as I am aware, the issue I raised in passing in my original *Monthly* article on Wilfred Burchett— the willingness of the Australian anti-communist camp to support, in one way or another, one of the great political crimes of the twentieth century, the Indonesian mass murder of 1965–6, where approximately as many died as in the Armenian genocide of 1915 or in the

Rwanda genocide of 1994—has never before been discussed by anyone associated with the anticommunist camp.

Unlike Manne, Henderson did not write a preface. This is from one of his emails:

You should not feel worried that you are taking up more of my 'valuable time'. It's just that—unlike you—I do not have a tenured job per courtesy of the Australian taxpayer. Consequently, I have to ration my time … I don't know what's going on at the La Trobe University Politics Department but you seem to have moved into psychic mode. It's as if John Edward (of 'Cross Country' fame) has become a visiting professor and influenced you. How could you possibly be 'pretty certain' of what 'both Santamaria and Knopelmacher would have been willing to discuss' about Indonesia more than a decade after their deaths? And how could you possibly know that 'Knopfelmacher would have been highly amused' about anything at all—since he is not with us any more? I note that you are now using invented positions of Franta in order to condemn Franta. This is grossly unprofessional and you should know better. It seems that you have taken to verballing the dead.

According to blogger Jack Marx, this 'grumble in the jungle' was 'an industrial strength stroke-fest that would have worn the chins off Mount Rushmore'. I regularly read both of the journals in which these exchanges appeared and was astonished that apparently neither Henderson nor Manne had stopped to wonder if the publication of this material was in the public interest. I can't understand how each could have felt so certain of his own rightness and of the value of his own opinion that he was prepared to move so many pages of argument from the private inbox to the public domain.

The twelfth-century French philosopher Pierre Abelard was a man who doubted almost everything except his passion for

Heloise. Their love story is one of the most famous in history. The lovers—teacher and student—were separated by Heloise's vindictive uncle. Abelard became a monk, and Heloise a nun. Although they were apart for the rest of their lives, their affair endured through love letters.

Over time, Abelard's relationship with Heloise has overshadowed his considerable intellectual achievements. In his day, he was revered as a significant teacher, philosopher and theologian. Abelard taught his students that the path to truth lay in the systematic application of doubt. Not only should doubt be brought to bear on external issues, but it should also be turned inward to test one's own assumptions. Abelard preferred statements of proof and fact rather than those relying on faith and rhetoric alone. He did not accept that something was true or right merely because somebody in leadership said it was so. As a result, he was targeted by authorities and frequently charged with heresy.

Like Abelard, many great thinkers throughout history have been branded heretics for publicly voicing scepticism. Those who have sought truth—be they philosophers or scientists, artists or writers, revolutionaries or explorers—have always begun their quests from a premise of doubt, not certainty. Their questions have most often run counter to the prevailing wisdom or authorities of the day. Copernicus asked whether the earth really was at the centre of the universe. Martin Luther asked whether the Roman Catholic Church's teaching on salvation was biblical. Thomas Jefferson asked why Americans couldn't govern themselves. Mary Wollstonecraft asked why women shouldn't have equal rights. Nelson Mandela asked why blacks weren't entitled to the same privileges as whites. To this day, science and philosophy are based on the notion that ideas and theories must be tested to see if they have foundation beyond plain faith. The scientific method takes it even further, proving theories by striving to disprove them.

That is why I am so alarmed by the influence of 'opinion'—with its basis in certainty—on the mainstream media.

It flies in the face of historical experience, which has shown again and again that the application of a doubtful mind is the best way to wisdom and insight. That principle is enshrined in journalism's foundations—objectivity and balance—yet today, some media organisations are drifting from those moorings in favour of reporting with unapologetic ideological bias. Fox News is the best known example of this, although we also see it in talk radio, blogs, newspaper columns and on cable television talk shows, such as *Lou Dobbs Tonight* on CNN. It's sometimes referred to as 'viewer cocooning' or 'niche news'. It preaches to the choir, telling consumers what they want to hear by pandering to their existing beliefs and biases.

Openly partisan journalism takes the view that objectivity is unattainable, so biases might as well be admitted rather than hidden. The logic is that those who watch the right-wing Fox News know they are getting news with a particular slant, as opposed to the viewers of the ABC, the BBC and CNN, who are told they are getting the objective truth. Critics claim that those organisations have a left-wing bias but just refuse to admit it.

In the USA, the free-to-air network NBC sticks to traditional, objective journalism, while its cable counterpart, MSNBC, takes a more opinion-oriented approach. Last year, a *New Yorker* profile of the MSNBC polemicist Keith Olbermann dissected the tension between the two arms of the NBC organisation. If Olbermann represented 'viewer cocooning', then Tim Russert, the highly regarded face of *Meet the Press* until his death in June 2008, represented the old style of reporting of which I am an advocate. Russert told the profile's writer:

> What cable emphasises, more and more, is opinion, or even advocacy. Whether it's Bill O'Reilly or Keith Olbermann or Lou Dobbs, that's what that particular platform or venue does. It's not what I do. What I do is different. I try very, very hard not to come up and say to people, 'This is what I believe', or 'This is good', or 'This is bad'. But rather, 'This is what I'm learning in my reporting', or 'This is what my analysis shows

> based on my reporting'. And as long as I
> can do that, I'm very, very comfortable.

I share Russert's view. I accept that no reporter can be perfectly objective—every day, every story involves subjective judgements—but if we give up striving for objectivity, if we stop examining ourselves for closed mindedness, then all is lost. A reader or viewer can no longer trust that the reporting is fair.

Newspaper journalists, even those on publications that strive for objectivity, can't help but note that it is now opinion writers who frequently have the highest profiles and often earn more money for less work. There is no doubt the best opinion writers truly provide genuine insight—commentators such as Fareed

Zakaria at *Newsweek*, Tom Friedman at the *New York Times*, and in Australia, Laura Tingle at the *Australian Financial Review* and Laurie Oakes at the *Daily Telegraph*. These journalists and many others like them use fact and calm analysis to make their cases, frequently offering useful historical or philosophical context and often breaking news as well.

More mediocre minds find it easier to sit at a desk and hammer out 800 words of vitriol than to beat the pavement, hit the phone, conduct countless interviews and conjure a story out of nothing. I look at the brave, difficult Australian journalism done by reporters such as Paul Toohey and Tony Koch at the *Australian*, or by Paul McGeough at the *Sydney Morning*

Herald: the comforts forgone in difficult regions, the risks to personal safety, the interviews with traumatised people, the dogged pursuit of important issues, year after year. That type of reporting takes courage, tenacity and sacrifice. It costs newspapers a lot more than opinion pieces do. Is it any surprise that some journalists and editors might find opinion writing more appealing than news reporting? Who wants to be Walt Bogdanich or Jake Hooker when you can be Maureen Dowd? If you've not heard of Bogdanich and Hooker, they won the 2008 Pulitzer Prize for investigative reporting. Point made.

The growth of cable television and radio, and the arrival of the internet have indisputably stimulated debate. The cacophony of blogs, programs, forums and websites offers a whole range of new viewpoints. There are vibrant conversations going on in all sorts of arenas, about all sorts of issues involving people who have previously never had an outlet for their opinions or expertise. That can only be good for democracy. But the new media are also full of echo chambers in which people immerse themselves in views that simply reflect and reinforce their own. The most strident participants in these conversations can be intolerant of different views. In 2008, George Megalogenis, an excellent, evidence-driven journalist at the *Australian* newspaper, took the unusual step of telling readers of his blog, *Meganomics*, that he would no longer publish abusive comments, even if it caused the blog to shut down for lack of traffic:

My mind is open on pretty much every issue. It's what journalists do for a living: keep their minds open in the hope that they catch the next new idea out there. Sadly, what a significant minority of my bloggers do is begin their posts with an assumption that everyone who disagrees with them is a 'moron' ... Talk to your fellow blogger as an equal, not as someone to belittle. Your ego may crave the sustenance that comes with abusing others. But trust me, it doesn't make for good reading. Beyond Mungo MacCallum and Hunter S Thompson, there are very few writers in the political sphere that have ever done abuse as poetry. I love their work; I often yawn at some of yours—no disrespect; it's just how I see things.

If readers and viewers stop wanting to hear opinions different from their own, and if journalists stop keeping their own views out of their reporting, how is this going to end? If this trend towards certainty reaches its extreme, and if 'niche news' rather than 'objective journalism' becomes the prevailing approach, I fear that to remain employable, I might be expected to pick a particular 'side' and report from it, keeping all my doubts and questions to myself. I don't see how that is compatible with an honest life.

III

One day last May, while preparing for an interview with the Australian Treasurer, Wayne Swan, I came across an anecdote that made my mouth fall open in surprise:

Swan was asked by Norah, a student, if he had ever experienced self-doubt. He had. 'I think all people in life go through that and the most important thing is to be honest about it', he told Brisbane

ABC Radio listeners. 'If you are experiencing self-doubt, it means that you are aware of vulnerabilities and sometimes I think that might be a bit better than people who just assume confidence in everything they do, full steam ahead.'

Swan's frankness stunned me because it is incredibly rare to hear a politician admit such a thing. Even more so than in the media, doubt equals weakness in politics. The politician who expresses doubt is seen as indecisive rather than capable of nuanced thought and self-reflection. By contrast, certainty is considered a strength. The leader who acts from unwavering confidence appears forceful and trustworthy. That is why statements such as Sarah Palin's 'you can't blink' are far more commonplace than Swan's admission of self-doubt.

In an environment that transforms normal emotion into weakness, many of our politicians develop a pervasive fear of saying anything that might reveal a chink in their armour and hand ammunition to opponents. They have concluded that honest or direct answers are a risk generally not worth taking. All but the most courageous choose to hide behind a wall of excessive media management.

In turn, their heavily scripted and stage-managed performances lead voters to become disengaged and distrustful. There is a commonly held view that politicians never say anything 'real'.

The public craves authenticity, which is why gaffes or slips of the tongue attract so much attention: they make politicians seem human. So begins a vicious cycle, in which the public and the media want to be able to trust and relate to politicians, but attack them if they err, admit doubt or show weakness.

Of course politicians aren't blameless victims. They (and other public officials) share the responsibility for creating this environment: by exaggerating opponents' flaws, by opposing for the sake of opposing, by often refusing to submit to even basic standards of scrutiny. Many politicians willingly manipulate the media to further their own ambitions or avoid legitimate accountability. Yet there are those politicians who, despite the risks of plain speaking, buck the trend towards excessive control. They have the courage to refuse, or are perhaps just unable to be bland or safe. These politicians tend to be portrayed in four ways: as disenfranchised, as gaffe-prone, as mavericks or as strong leaders.

The former Australian Opposition leader Mark Latham is the classic example of the disenfranchised politician who speaks his mind. With the release of *The Latham Diaries*, he let loose on almost everybody in his own party and on many others. This is the politician who no longer has anything to lose and so has nothing to fear.

The US Vice President, Joseph Biden, represents the gaffe-prone politician, who seems to think aloud a little too often. During Barack Obama's presidential bid, Biden guaranteed that the world would 'test' Obama with a major crisis during his first six months in office, giving opponents a chance to fear-monger. He also talked about Franklin Delano Roosevelt watching television during the Great Depression (television was not publicly available until years later). Australia's former foreign minister Alexander Downer displayed a tendency for gaffes early in his career (most famously his 'things that batter' gag about domestic violence). Once in government, however, Downer managed to turn his foot-in-mouth propensity into a reputation for being comparatively forthright.

John McCain is the maverick arche-
type: the outspoken, independent-minded
politician who will not necessarily toe the
party line. Mavericks tend to be beloved of
the media and the public because they are
engaging and unpredictable. They often
play useful roles in keeping governments
and oppositions accountable. Australian
examples include Barnaby Joyce, Bob
Katter and Brian Harradine. Mavericks
do well on the periphery of politics but
sometimes not in positions of leadership,
where they can find it hard to compromise
and hold their tongues.

Strong leaders are those who are able to
speak their minds frankly and carry others
along with them. The former Australian
prime minister John Howard was one who

could take a difficult, unpopular policy, such as a goods and services tax, and, through force of will, persuade a majority of voters to support him. Strong leaders trust instinct and often find themselves loved and loathed in equal parts. John Howard's predecessor, Paul Keating, and former British prime minister Margaret Thatcher join him in this category.

More than any other breed of frank politician, strong leaders demonstrate the electoral benefit of certainty. They don't 'blink', as Sarah Palin put it, and the public equates that certainty with honesty, loyalty, reliability and determination (at least until the public falls out of love and begins to equate it with stubbornness or egomania). We're all familiar with the compliments such leaders attract: 'You always knew what he stood for'; 'She went down fighting'; 'He knew what he believed in'. Yet for all their appeal, strong leadership and unshakeable self-confidence have their pitfalls. No political reign of recent times demonstrates this more amply than the presidency of George W Bush.

The philosophical foundation of George Bush's presidency was straightforward: moral certainty and a reliance on 'gut'. Beginning in 2002, the Republican gave journalist Bob Woodward unprecedented access for the first of four books on the

Bush administration. The President explained what would sustain his eight years in the White House:

> First of all, a president has got to be the calcium in the backbone. If I weaken, the whole team weakens. If I'm doubtful, I can assure you there will be a lot of doubt. If my confidence level in our ability declines, it will send ripples throughout the whole organisation. I mean, it's essential that we be confident and determined and united.

Bush also placed an extraordinary amount of faith in his gut instinct. As Woodward notes in *Bush at War*:

> During the interview, the president spoke a dozen times about his 'instincts'

or his 'instinctive' reactions, including his statement, 'I'm not a textbook player, I'm a gut player.' It's pretty clear that Bush's role as politician, president and commander in chief is driven by a secular faith in his instincts—his natural and spontaneous conclusions and judgements. His instincts are almost his second religion.

Bush relied on body language and the 'vibe' people gave him. According to Woodward, at a meeting with General Tommy Franks in the planning stage for the Iraq war, Bush mostly relied on Franks's demeanour in evaluating the usefulness of his advice. He also decided he could trust Russian President Vladimir Putin based on gut feeling. 'I looked the man in the eye', Bush said after their first meeting in 2001. 'I found him to be very straightforward and trustworthy and we had a very good dialogue. I was able to get a sense of his soul.'

Bush also wanted certainty in his advisors: 'I don't need people around me who are not steady … And if there's kind of a hand-wringing attitude going on when times are tough, I don't like it'. Over time, this attitude meant that many administration officials grew reluctant to contradict the President or offer alternative views. Open dialogue and debate were not desirable because they implied the unsteadiness that Bush disliked. As the former *Wall Street Journal* reporter Ron Suskind notes, a culture of cockiness developed from the top down: if the President doesn't second-guess himself, why should we?

In October 2004, Suskind wrote a lengthy article examining Bush's lack of doubt. He interviewed many officials about White House culture and concluded that there was 'a disdain for contemplation or deliberation, an embrace of decisiveness, a retreat from empiricism, a sometimes bullying impatience with doubters and even friendly questioners'. The president of the conservative American Enterprise Institute, Christopher DeMuth, told Suskind, 'It's a too tightly managed decision-making process. When they make decisions, a very small number of people are in the room, and it has a certain effect of constricting the range of alternatives being offered'.

DeMuth was not the only concerned Republican. Treasury Secretary Paul O'Neill, counter-terrorism tsar Richard Clarke, Deputy Secretary of State Richard Armitage and CIA Director George Tenet were among those who ultimately found the environment unproductive. A former advisor to Ronald Reagan and George HW Bush, Bruce Bartlett, said, 'Bush dispenses with people who confront him with inconvenient facts … absolute faith like that overwhelms a need for analysis. The whole thing about faith is to believe things for which there is no empirical evidence'.

There were various theories about the source of Bush's unshakeable certainty. One was his religious faith and a tendency to believe he was on a mission from God. A second was that Bush never developed self-doubt because he had never had to confront his own weaknesses. When he had failed in life, his family had always bailed him out. A third reason was that having seen his father pilloried for a lack of direction during the first Bush presidency, the younger Bush had decided that unwavering vision was all-important. Anything that detracted from it needed to be excised.

Bush's reliance on 'gut' is not without merit. One of the best-selling books of 2005 was *Blink: The Power of Thinking without Thinking* by Malcolm Gladwell. As its subtitle indicates, it explores the value of relying on instinct rather than conscious thought. Gladwell's thesis is that if a person has a lot of knowledge or experience in a field, a snap judgement can be more effective than lengthy analysis. Gladwell explains the concept of 'thin slicing', the ability of the unconscious to use past experience to identify patterns in current situations and behaviour. Using 'thin slicing', the so-called 'adaptive unconscious' allows people to make perfect decisions in the blink of an eye, seemingly going by 'gut' rather than reason.

A case study in *Blink* focuses on one of the world's top tennis coaches, Vic Braden. Braden had more than fifty years' experience playing and coaching tennis at elite levels, and he could predict with almost 100 per cent accuracy when any player was about to double-fault. As the player threw the ball up and raised the racquet, Braden could not consciously explain his reasoning; he just instinctively knew, in that split second, that it would be a double-fault. Through experience, Braden's brain was so attuned to the ingredients of a good serve, that his 'adaptive unconscious'—or 'gut'—took over.

Once somebody reaches this level of expertise, conscious thought—including self-doubt—becomes a hindrance rather than a help. It derails instinct. From the age of ten, I have played the piano. When I am learning a new piece of music, the early practice requires a great deal of concentration. I consciously think about which fingers are going to strike which notes. I count beats in my head. My eyes are glued to the notes on the page in front of me. I play the piece over and over again for hours. Then one day, seemingly in an instant, something changes. I can play the music without thinking about it. Often, I no longer need the sheet music. The hands move together seamlessly, and the timing seems instinctive. The 'adaptive unconscious' kicks in. My gut takes control. My fingers are so practised that they seem to know what to do on their own without my brain's help.

It's at this point that over-thinking becomes a problem. Once my 'gut' is dominant, if I start consciously thinking about the mechanics of playing the piece, I can no longer do it. My fingers turn into useless sausages that no longer know where to go. If I begin to indulge self-doubt—*Here comes the hardest part ... I hope I can do it ... Do I use my third or fourth finger here?*—invariably, I crash. It reminds me of the scene in *Star Wars* in which Obi-Wan Kenobi advises Luke Skywalker to 'use the force'. Once the work has been done to reach a 'gut' level of expertise, the most important thing is to relax so that the analytic part of the brain doesn't derail the instinctive part. For a long time, I didn't know how to describe the strange effect over-thinking had on my music. I didn't even realise that it affected anyone else until I told my husband about it. 'Oh you mean the yips', he said. He and his brother had also studied piano as children and had picked up the term 'the yips' to refer to the experience of sabotaging their own performance by thinking too hard about it.

George Bush did not have the yips. He was not at risk of over-thinking because he was not prone to doubt or second-guess himself, nor did he like endlessly mulling over options. Bush's problem was an over-reliance on instinct. Unlike Vic Braden, Bush's gut was not developed from experience, so it was not reliable. He had never been President before; he had never gone to war before; he had never responded to a terrorist attack before. As such, Bush was not a good candidate for 'thin slicing'. Reason, intellect and fact would have been better guides than instinct.

The failure of Bush's gut—and the drawback of certainty as an intellectual or political premise—is evident in the results of his presidency: a nation in recession and possibly on the brink of depression, two unfinished wars abroad, a resurgent al Qaeda and Taliban on the Pakistan border, a $400 billion federal budget deficit, serious anti-Americanism abroad and a presidential approval rating among history's lowest.

Would things have been different if Bush had listened more to facts instead of his gut? Would his administration have made fewer mistakes had he fostered a culture of open debate? Would Bush have been a better President had he occasionally wondered if he were wrong?

Despite the obvious traps of certainty, a political leader who shows doubt is more likely to be slaughtered by opponents and the media. Politics is littered with the carcases of the indecisive. There are the over-thinkers, such as the former Democratic presidential candidate John Kerry, who could not shake the tag of 'flip-flopper' during the 2004 US election. Then there are the politically expedient. The tendency to switch courses looking for political advantage was one of the major factors in the ousting of former Australian Opposition leader Brendan Nelson.

During July 2008, Nelson repeatedly backflipped on the Coalition's climate-change policy, specifically over whether the Opposition should support the government's plan for an emissions trading scheme. Nelson went from unconditionally supporting the implementation of such a scheme in 2012 to making the start date conditional on international action. He then reverted to the original position when he couldn't win the support of his shadow cabinet. But then he switched course yet again—only a day later—when his backbench signalled that it preferred the conditional policy.

Although Nelson's reasons were partly economic and environmental, he was also driven by raw politics: the desire to differentiate the Coalition from the ALP, and to find the Rudd government's Achilles heel. Nelson—and some of his advisors—believed that during an economic downturn, the public would turn against the government when an emissions trading scheme started to take money out of their pockets. But Nelson's prevarication, at a time when his leadership was already floundering, was fatal.

The role of climate change in Nelson's downfall is instructive. The overwhelming weight of scientific evidence supports the existence of human-induced climate change. The most respected scientific bodies in the world are in agreement. Almost all of the world's political leaders accept the need for action. Those who choose to question the science or policies surrounding global warming are routinely derided as 'deniers' or 'heretics'. Instead, their views should be welcomed. Doubters have a very important role to play as the minority voice on an issue on which there is almost universal consensus. It is disappointing that the debate about climate change seems to have largely split down ideological lines, because that may inhibit productive discussion. But we do need people to challenge the prevailing orthodoxy. They will force our politicians and scientists to keep testing the evidence on climate change and exploring the policy options. It will lead to better outcomes for us all.

My ABC colleague, chief political correspondent Chris Uhlmann, beautifully encapsulated on the ABC's *Insiders* program why climate change requires a doubtful mind:

> As a former seminarian, one of the things that strikes me most strongly about this debate is its theological nature, and that's essentially that we have sinned against the environment, that we are now being punished and the only way that we can escape that punishment is to wear a hairshirt for the rest of our lives and hope that in the next life, and our children's lives, and our

children's children's lives, that things will get better.

Now, I am willing to sign up for that, but this is a very long caravan and there are a lot of lunatics that are attached to the end of it. I do not believe every proposition that's been put.

When the weather department can tell me what the weather is going to be like next Friday with any certainty and Treasury can get within a million dollars of what the surplus is going to be next year, I'll believe an economic model that marries those two things and casts them out over 100 years.

As Uhlmann understands, the best way to approach this issue, both in scientific and policy terms, is to apply the scientific method: try to disprove the proposition and see if it still holds up. If we do this, there is everything to gain and nothing to lose. 'When men are most sure and arrogant,' Scottish philosopher David Hume wrote more than two hundred years ago, 'they are most commonly mistaken, giving views to passion without that proper deliberation which alone can secure them from the grossest absurdities'.

When politicians or journalists or commentators make doubt seem like heresy or stupidity, whether the issue is climate change or anything else, it sends a message to us all. It says: if you experience second thoughts or feel less than certain and confident in your own opinions at all times, you are weak. It encourages a culture of dishonesty in which we feel scared to show our humanity for fear of derision.

We don't all make decisions that affect the entire nation or world, as politicians do. But we do face our own unique challenges every day: we decide where to send our children to day-care or consider selling our houses or make presentations at work or give speeches at friends' weddings. *What if I can't do it? What if I muck this up? What if this is a disaster? What if I'm making the wrong choice?* These are natural, sensible and desirable thoughts. They prevent us from acting recklessly without regard for consequences. I don't think we should be made to feel inferior for having them or be ashamed to admit them.

IV

My Dad hasn't read Malcolm Gladwell. He probably hasn't heard of 'thin slicing' or the 'adaptive unconscious'. Yet for years, he has been giving me a piece of advice that shows he instinctively understands the concept. 'Daughter,' he says, affectionately slapping me on the back so hard I stumble forward, 'preparation and planning prevent piss-poor performance'.

This is a philosophy Dad continues to apply to everything in life, from paving a driveway to going camping. A few years ago, he was organising a six-week road trip with some mates, and he proudly showed me the spreadsheet he had prepared. It truly was an extraordinary feat of organisation, outlining everything from how many kilometres they would drive each day to what they'd be eating for breakfast and dinner. 'See daughter, look here', he said, pointing to the relevant column. 'On the 13th, we'll be in Cloncurry and we'll have rissoles for tea. Then from the 14th, we alternate sausages, baked beans, steak, fish and chips, pub dinner, and then we get back to rissoles.'

'But what if on the 13th nobody feels like rissoles?' I asked, channelling my inner eleven year old.

'What if nobody feels like rissoles?' Dad repeated incredulously, as if I had just asked where they'd be getting their pedicures. 'They'll bloody eat what they get, and they'll be bloody grateful for it.'

Dad might appear to be acting from a position of certainty by insisting that on the 13th they will be having rissoles. But in reality, through preparation and planning, he's making sure that any doubts he has about the trip going piss-poorly are put to rest. If he had a certain mind, rather than a doubtful one, he wouldn't wonder about what might happen if he were to find himself in the middle of nowhere on the 13th with nothing to eat. He wouldn't feel the need to do the preparation. I may poke fun at the roster, but I've never gone hungry or run out of petrol in Dad's company.

For obvious reasons, Dad prefers my attendance only on short camping trips. As long as I let him know what I'd like to eat three months in advance, we get along famously. Over the years, he's managed to find certain opportunities for fun—or perhaps payback—in my endless questions. 'Dad, what chance is there that I'll step on a snake?' I asked when we were walking through some bush at Mount Tambourine in early 2005.

'Almost bloody certain, daughter', he said firmly. 'Seven of the ten deadliest snakes in the world live in the Queensland bush. You'd better watch out for the hoop snake. You'll never survive if you see one of them.'

'The hoop snake?' I responded with trepidation. 'What's that?'

'It's this bloody vicious little bugger', he went on. 'See most snakes, if they hear you coming, they'll go away, but the hoop snake is aggressive and he rolls himself into a hoop, and if you start running, he starts rolling after you and then BAM'— Dad jabbed his hand out in front—'He strikes!'

Dad spent a significant part of his career training soldiers for jungle warfare, so he has a lot of credibility when it comes to the bush. I'm completely ignorant and a little scared of it. Based on his expertise and my discomfort, the threat of an angry hoop snake seemed entirely plausible. I fell for Dad's malarky in much the same way that he would unquestioningly take my word for it if I told him that *Catcher in the Rye* was about a baseball player working in a bread factory.

I spent the rest of that walk in terror of a hoop snake until, hours later, Dad finally cracked. 'You bloody squeezer,' he gasped through his laughter, 'I thought you were supposed to be some educated smart arse'.

'Give me strength!' I felt like spluttering.

I am always going to be a person who wonders *What if?* Even if I wanted to be more sure of myself, more certain of my own opinions, I wouldn't be able to manage it. I can't change who I am, and I'm fine with that. But I have learnt that a doubtful mind comes with two major drawbacks— three if you include your father's ability to traumatise you.

The first disadvantage is anxiety. Doubt seems to go hand in hand with worry, often unnecessary concern about things that are unlikely ever to happen. Every time I walk into the television studio to anchor *Lateline*, no matter how much preparation I've done, no matter how confident I am in my own experience, no matter that I've done it many times previously, I still have the same sinking feeling of dread and the same thought: *Oh God, I've left it too late to leave.*

The second drawback is a lack of all-consuming passion. It is difficult to be passionate about anything when I question everything. I have things that I love to do in life, but I don't really feel that anything is a matter of life and death. I love playing the piano, and if tomorrow I no longer had that ability, I would be devastated. But I wouldn't rather be dead. I love being a journalist. I'd be gutted if I had to change jobs. But I'm sure I'd find something else. I believe in the adage 'hard work pays off' with great conviction. But if somebody were to disagree with me on that, I wouldn't feel the need to write a column deriding them for their incomprehensible stupidity.

I envy people with great passion and wonder what it might be like. About ten years ago, I covered a press conference that left a strong impression on me. It wasn't a famous story—in fact, I can't even remember the specifics of it. The New South Wales Greens MP Ian Cohen had called a media event to respond to an environmental announcement by the state government. Nothing sticks in my memory except that Cohen was struggling to hold back tears. With the greatest sincerity and urgency in his voice, he begged, absolutely begged, the premier to reverse course. Cohen obviously cared so passionately that he made me feel almost melancholy. *Wow*, I thought to myself, *I wish I cared that much about something*. I would like to ask Abelard why he never doubted his passion for Heloise from the day he met her, while he relentlessly questioned everything else in life.

I look at people who are particularly self-assured or laid-back or passionate and I envy them. But if I had the opportunity to trade in my personality and rid myself of doubt, I don't think I would. I like the ability to question myself and everything else. I feel that without a doubtful mind, I wouldn't learn as much or have as much fun. But I could be wrong.

Notes

Part I

Page 9: Kevin Rudd's alleged 'Pine Rivers' remark is quoted in M Latham, 'Rewarding Bad Behaviour', *Australian Financial Review*, 15 May 2008, p. 86.

Part II

Page 16: For Sarah Palin's first interview, see C Gibson, interview with Sarah Palin, *World News*, television program, ABC America, 11 September 2008, transcript viewed December 2008, <abcnews.go.com/politics/vote2008/Story?id=5782924&page=1>.

Page 21: David Frum's comments on Sarah Palin's unsuitability for the presidency are quoted in A Nagourney, 'Concern about Palin's Readiness as the

Big Test Nears'. *New York Times*, 29 September 2008, viewed December 2008, <www.nytimes.com/2008/09/30/us/politics/30palin.htm>.

Pages 22–3: For Melanie Phillips's views on Sarah Palin, see M Phillips, 'Contempt, Apathy and Lies: Why Britain Is Crying Out for Our Own Pitbull with Lipstick', *Daily Mail*, 8 September 2008, viewed December 2008, <www.dailymail.co.uk/news/article-1053331/Contempt-apathy-lies---Britain-crying-pitbull-lipstick.html>.

Pages 23–4: For Maureen Dowd's views on Sarah Palin, see M Dowd, 'Vice in Go-Go Boots?', *New York Times*, 31 August 2008, viewed December 2008, <www.nytimes.com/2008/08/31/opinion/31dowd.html>.

Pages 27–8: Hendrik Hertzberg's comment on political ideology can be found in H Hertzberg, 'A Moral Ideologue', in *On Politics: Observations and Arguments*, Penguin, New York, 2004, p. 56.

Pages 29–30: Norman Mailer's letter to William F Buckley is reproduced in N Mailer, 'In the Ring', *New Yorker*, 6 October 2008, pp. 51–63.

Page 31: Christopher Buckley's first endorsement of Obama can be found at C Buckley, 'Sorry, Dad, I'm Voting for Obama', *Daily Beast*, viewed December 2008, <www.thedailybeast.com/blogs-

and-stories/2008-10-10/the-conservative-case-for-obama>.

Page 32: Christopher Buckley's follow-up blog can be found at C Buckley, 'Buckley Bows Out of *National Review*', *Daily Beast*, viewed December 2008, <www.thedailybeast.com/blogs-and-stories/2008-10-14/sorry-dad-i-was-fired>.

Page 33: Robert Manne's original essay on Wilfred Burchett is R Manne, 'Agent of Influence: Reassessing Wilfred Burchett', *Monthly*, no. 35, June 2008, viewed December 2008, <www.themonthly.com.au/tm/node/1015>.

Page 34: For the *Australian*'s reporting of the Manne–Henderson spat, see C Overington, 'Writers Brawl at Length over a Few Cross Words', *Australian*, 6 September 2008, viewed December 2008, <www.theaustralian.news.com.au/story/0,25197,24302146-13480,00.html>.

Pages 34–6: For Robert Manne's version of the spat with Gerard Henderson, see R Manne, 'Apologetics and Hypocrisy', *Monthly*, online edition only, viewed December 2008, <www.themonthly.com.au/tm/node/1169>.

Pages 36–7: For Gerard Henderson's version of the spat with Robert Manne, see G Henderson, 'Robert Manne sans Evidence', *Sydney Institute Quarterly*, no. 33, August 2008, pp. 36–42, viewed December 2008, <www.thesydneyinstitute.com.au/downloads/SIQ33.pdf>.

Pages 37–8: Jack Marx's take on the Henderson–Manne row can be found at J Marx, 'Manne v Henderson: The Grumble in the Jungle', *Jack Marx Live Blog*, viewed December 2008, <blogs.news.com.au/jackmarxlive/index.php/news/comments/the_grumble_in_the_jungle/>.

Pages 44–5: Tim Russert's description of his style of reporting is quoted in PJ Boyer, 'One Angry Man: Is Keith Olbermann Changing TV News?' *New Yorker*, 23 June 2008, viewed January 2009, <www.newyorker.com/reporting/2008/06/23/080623fa_fact_boyer?currentPage=all>.

Pages 48–50: The George Megalogenis quote can be found at G Megalogenis, 'What Next?', *Meganomics Blog*, 20 August 2008, viewed December 2008, <blogs.theaustralian.news.com.au/meganomics/index.php/theaustralian/comments/what_next/>.

Part III

Pages 51–52: Wayne Swan's admission of self-doubt is quoted in T Dusevic, 'True Brew and Serious Hip-Pocket Nerve', *Australian Financial Review*, 30 May 2008, p. 73.

Page 59: On George W Bush's certainty, see B Woodward, *State of Denial*, Simon & Schuster, New York, 2006; B Woodward, *Plan of Attack*, Simon & Schuster, New York, 2004; B Woodward, *Bush at War*, Simon & Schuster, New York, 2002; BBC News, 'Bush and Putin: Best of Friends', *BBC News Online*, 16 June 2001, viewed December 2008, <news.bbc.co.uk/2/hi/europe/1392791.stm>; R Suskind, 'Faith, Certainty and the Presidency of George W Bush', *New York Times Magazine*, 17 October 2004, viewed January 2009, <www.nytimes.com/2004/10/17/magazine/17BUSH.html>.

Pages 65–7: On split-second judgements, see M Gladwell, *Blink: The Power of Thinking without Thinking*, Little, Brown & Company, New York, 2005.

Pages 76–7: For Chris Uhlmann's comments on climate change scepticism, see C Uhlmann, 'The Week in Politics', *Insiders*, television program, ABC TV, 6 July 2008, transcript viewed December 2008, <www.abc.net.au/insiders/content/2007/s2295607.htm>.

Leigh Sales is a Walkley Award–winning journalist who anchors ABC TV's *Lateline* program on Wednesday, Thursday and Friday nights. She has held senior positions at the network including national security correspondent and Washington correspondent. Her first book, *Detainee 002: The Case of David Hicks*, won the 2007 George Munster Award for Independent Journalism and was shortlisted for the 2008 Victorian Premier's Literary Prize.

Little Books on Big Themes

Germaine Greer ON RAGE
Blanche d'Alpuget ON LONGING
Barrie Kosky ON ECSTASY
David Malouf ON EXPERIENCE

Don Watson ON INDIGNATION
Malcolm Knox ON OBSESSION
Gay Bilson ON DIGESTION
Anne Summers ON LUCK

Robert Dessaix ON HUMBUG
Julian Burnside ON PRIVILEGE
Elisabeth Wynhausen ON RESILIENCE
Susan Johnson ON BEAUTY

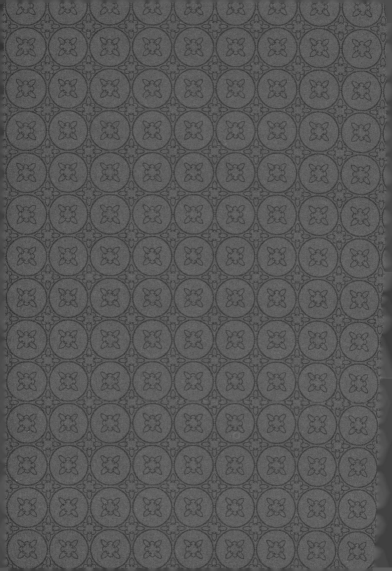